Progress-Monitoring Assessments

Grade 5

HOUGHTON MIFFLIN HARCOURT

Contents

Progress-Monitoring Assessments

The *Houghton Mifflin Harcourt Journeys* program provides intervention to support students who are having difficulty reading. The Progress-Monitoring Assessments provide biweekly checks on students' progress. The fifteen oral tests are administered individually and assess students' growth in reading skills.

Purpose of the Progress-Monitoring Assessments

- To check on a student's growth or problems in learning skills and vocabulary
- To target learning gaps by using these test results combined with test results from the core instructional program

Skills Tested in the Intervention Program

Tested skills include
- Fluency (accuracy and rate)
- Comprehension
- Target Vocabulary

Test Organization

- Fifteen biweekly assessments are provided on blackline masters.

- Each assessment includes the student's test followed by the teacher's test form with questions and scoring information.

- This booklet provides directions for administering and scoring each test. Also included are guidelines for interpreting test results and reproducible record-keeping forms.

Progress-Monitoring Assessments have two sections:

- Passages for students to read aloud, which include selected Target Vocabulary from the previous two lessons

- Oral questions that check comprehension and vocabulary

Fluency goals are based on below grade-level norms in order to measure progress with intervention instruction. Use grade-level fluency norms, along with observation and program assessment, to determine whether or not a student can transition out of intervention.

Administering the Assessments

Administer each assessment orally to individuals approximately every two weeks. The test should take three to five minutes.

Prepare one student test form and a teacher's test form for each student being tested. Use it to record the student's responses and scores.

Materials Needed

- Student's test form
- Teacher's test form (one per student being tested)
- Stopwatch, watch, or clock with a second hand
- Clipboard (optional)

Keep in Mind

- Find a quiet area to conduct the test.

- Explain the task, and let the student know that you will be taking notes as he or she reads a passage aloud.

- Tell the student to read at his or her usual pace and not rush through the reading.

- Wait until the student has left to score and analyze the results.

To administer the oral reading section:

- Have a clock or watch with a second hand or a stopwatch available to time the student's reading.

- Explain that the test has two parts. First, you'll listen to the student read a passage aloud. Then you'll ask questions about it. If a student has trouble decoding a word, remind him or her to use the Decoding Strategy.

- Time the student's reading for 30 seconds.

- Record errors by drawing a line through mispronounced or omitted words. Write in words that the student inserts. Mark self-corrections with SC above the word.

- Mark an X on the last word that the student reads at 30 seconds.

- Allow the student to finish reading the entire passage.

To administer the comprehension and vocabulary questions:

- At the end of the reading ask the questions provided, and have the student respond orally.

- Give the student a reasonable time to respond. Use the rubric on the teacher's test form to evaluate the response. Record a number.

Scoring the Assessments

1. Determine the student's fluency score; record it on the teacher's test form.

- Count mispronunciations, additions, and omissions as errors.

- Do not count repetitions or self-corrections as errors.

- Subtract errors from total number of words read to get the total number of words read correctly in 30 seconds.

- Multiply the words read correctly in 30 seconds times 2 to determine the number of words read correctly in one minute (WCPM).

2. Calculate the student's comprehension and vocabulary score. Record it on the teacher's test form.

How to Score Comprehension and Vocabulary Questions
2 = full credit answer
1 = partial credit answer
0 = incorrect/unanswered

- Evaluate the completeness of the student's answers. Give partial credit for an answer with too few details or one that required prompting. Record the number.

- Add the vocabulary and comprehension scores together and enter the total score.

3. Compare the scores and goals. Decide whether the student should move ahead or needs reteaching.

4. Record each student's scores across test periods on the Progress-Monitoring Chart. See the blackline masters on pages xi–xii.

Interpreting Test Results

Use progress-monitoring test results, observations, and grade-level assessment results to make decisions about future intervention. They will help you:

- determine if the student needs additional intervention or can be transitioned back to core instruction only

- evaluate the overall effectiveness of intervention strategies by noting sufficient progress and learning

- adjust skill instruction to address specific learning gaps

Consider how a student's scores compare to the goals. Decide if the student is benefiting from additional intervention.

☐ **Move Ahead** The student met goals for both sections.	☐ **Needs Reteaching** The student did not meet goals for one or both sections.

Adjusting Instruction

Evaluate a student's errors and responses to identify problem areas and starting points for reteaching, review, and extra practice.

- **To build accuracy** Analyze the types of errors in oral reading. Reteach target phonics/decoding skills as needed, and provide appropriate word lists for more practice. If a student is making many self-corrections, try recording the student's reading and play it back so he or she can hear his or her own reading.

- **To build fluency** Provide familiar texts at a student's independent reading level for repeated or coached readings.

- **To build comprehension** Emphasize understanding the meaning of text. Take turns with students modeling how to apply comprehension strategies to different texts.

Test Results and Regrouping

Students in Strategic Intervention take part in the core instruction, activities, and assessments from *Houghton Mifflin Harcourt Journeys*. Test results from the Progress-Monitoring Assessments and Quick Check observations from the lessons indicate whether a student is benefiting from Strategic Intervention. Test results from other *Journeys* assessments provide data to help determine how to regroup students periodically.

Using *Houghton Mifflin Harcourt Journeys* Assessments	
Core Instructional Program Weekly and Unit Tests Benchmark and Fluency Tests	• Measure grade-level skill mastery and growth. • Use cut-off scores and professional judgment to regroup students who need intervention support.
Strategic Intervention Biweekly Progress-Monitoring Assessments	• Measures a student's gains as a result of Strategic Intervention instruction. • Use progress-monitoring results, observations, and program assessments to determine if a student needs additional Strategic Intervention or should transition out of intervention or to more intensive intervention. • If a student has not performed adequately (met goals) for two or three consecutive assessments, consult with colleagues to decide whether to increase the intensity of intervention.

Progress-Monitoring Chart

Name _____ Teacher _____ School year _____

Enter scores from test forms.

For Lessons	FLUENCY		COMPREHENSION and VOCABULARY	ACTIONS (Check One)		COMMENTS
	Date Given	Enter Words Correct per Minute (WCPM)	Enter Score Goal: 4/6	Move Ahead	Needs Reteaching	
1–2						
3–4						
5–6						
7–8						
9–10						
11–12						
13–14						

Progress-Monitoring Chart

Name —————— Teacher —————— School year ——————

Enter scores from test forms.

For Lessons	Date Given	FLUENCY Enter Words Correct per Minute (WCPM)	COMPREHENSION and VOCABULARY Enter Score Goal: 4/6	ACTIONS (Check One)		COMMENTS
				Move Ahead	Needs Reteaching	
15–16						
17–18						
19–20						
21–22						
23–24						
25–26						
27–28						
29–30						

The Quick Save

Robert floated lazily on his back. He let the gentle ocean waves push him toward the shore, just a few yards away. The sky was a perfect blue, and the afternoon sun warmed the swimmers as they splashed in the surf. Soon it would be time for Robert and his sister Anna to go home, but he didn't let himself think of this. Instead, he was thinking how good it felt to be by himself and relax in the water.

Suddenly, a shout rudely interrupted his thoughts. He tried to ignore it, but the panic in the voice made this impossible. "Help, please help! Somebody help her!" the woman called.

"She's drowning!" someone else yelled.

At first, Robert's brain wouldn't function, so he couldn't tell what was happening. As his toes touched the sand, he heard Anna's urgent voice. "She's over there, Robert! Get her!" Anna was pointing to the waves nearby.

Looking around quickly, Robert watched as a child struggled to keep her head above water. Without another thought, he dove and reached for her. His fingers soon closed around a tiny arm. Grasping the girl with strong hands, Robert lifted her out of the water. His only thought now was for her safety. She coughed and then began to cry. With relief, Robert knew this meant she would be all right.

The Quick Save

	3

Robert floated lazily on his back. He let the gentle | 13

ocean waves push him toward the shore, just a few yards | 24

away. The sky was a perfect blue, and the afternoon sun | 35

warmed the swimmers as they splashed in the surf. Soon | 45

it would be time for Robert and his sister Anna to go | 57

home, but he didn't let himself think of this. Instead, he | 68

was thinking how good it felt to be by himself and relax | 80

in the water. | 83

Suddenly, a shout rudely interrupted his thoughts. | 90

He tried to ignore it, but the panic in the voice made | 102

this impossible. "Help, please help! Somebody help | 109

her!" the woman called. | 113

"She's drowning!" someone else yelled. | 118

At first, Robert's brain wouldn't function, so he | 126

couldn't tell what was happening. As his toes touched | 135

the sand, he heard Anna's urgent voice. "She's over | 144

there, Robert! Get her!" Anna was pointing to the | 153

waves nearby. | 155

Looking around quickly, Robert watched as a | 162

child struggled to keep her head above water. Without | 171

another thought, he dove and reached for her. His | 180

fingers soon closed around a tiny arm. Grasping the girl | 190

with strong hands, Robert lifted her out of the water. | 200

His only thought now was for her safety. She coughed | 210

and then began to cry. With relief, Robert knew this | 220

meant she would be all right. | 226

GO ON

Comprehension and Vocabulary Questions

1. *What does Robert do in this story?* (Robert saves a girl from drowning.)

2. *What happens when a shout underlines interrupts Robert's thoughts?* (Robert is feeling good on the water. Then the shout makes him pay attention to the girl's cries.)

3. *How does Robert know that the girl is all right?* (She coughs and begins to cry.)

Fluency Score	**Comprehension/Vocabulary Score**	**How to Score Questions**
Total words correctly read in 30 seconds _____ X 2	1. _____	2 = full credit answer
	2. _____	1 = partial credit answer
Score _____	3. _____	0 = incorrect/unanswered
Goal 61–81 WCPM	Score _____ /6 Goal = 4/6	

☐ **Move Ahead** The student met goals for both sections.	☐ **Needs Reteaching** The student did not meet goals for one or both sections.

Two Ground Birds

Have you ever seen the Road Runner in a cartoon? A roadrunner is a real bird. Unlike many birds, roadrunners prefer running to flying. There are other desert birds that prefer the ground to the air, too. One of these is the Gambel's quail. Let's take a closer look at these two ground birds.

Roadrunners live throughout the Southwest. These birds are not easily intimidated. They can run at speeds of 15 miles per hour or more. So, they can outrun most enemies. From their head to their long tail, they can grow to 22 inches. Like many birds, they eat spiders and insects. They also eat lizards and snakes. Roadrunners have never hesitated to get a meal from other birds. They eat the eggs of these birds. Sometimes they even eat baby birds.

Quails also live mainly on the ground. They build their nests and look for food there. The Gambel's quail, like the roadrunner, lives in the Southwest. However, its range does not go as far into Texas as the roadrunner's. This quail grows to about 10 inches long. Like other quails, it has a short tail. It also has a pretty red head and a black topnotch that curls towards its face. Quails eat mainly seeds and berries, but they can eat insects. Sometimes they change their routine and eat an occasional egg. What a delicacy!

Two Ground Birds

Have you ever seen the Road Runner in a cartoon? 13

A roadrunner is a real bird. Unlike many birds, 22

roadrunners prefer running to flying. There are other 30

desert birds that prefer the ground to the air, too. One 41

of these is the Gambel's quail. Let's take a closer look at 53

these two ground birds. 57

Roadrunners live throughout the Southwest. These 63

birds are not easily intimidated. They can run at speeds 73

of 15 miles per hour or more. So, they can outrun most 85

enemies. From their head to their long tail, they can 95

grow to 22 inches. Like many birds, they eat spiders and 106

insects. They also eat lizards and snakes. Roadrunners 114

have never hesitated to get a meal from other birds. 124

They eat the eggs of these birds. Sometimes they even 134

eat baby birds. 137

Quails also live mainly on the ground. They build 146

their nests and look for food there. The Gambel's quail, 156

like the roadrunner, lives in the Southwest. However, its 165

range does not go as far into Texas as the roadrunner's. 176

This quail grows to about 10 inches long. Like other 186

quails, it has a short tail. It also has a pretty red head 199

and a black topnotch that curls towards its face. Quails 209

eat mainly seeds and berries, but they can eat insects. 219

Sometimes they change their routine and eat an 227

occasional egg. What a delicacy! 232

3

GO ON

Name _____ Date _____

Comprehension and Vocabulary Questions

1. *What is unusual about roadrunners and quails?* (Both birds prefer to run instead of fly.)

2. *Why are roadrunners not easily <u>intimidated</u> by enemies?* (Roadrunners are not easily intimidated because they can outrun most of their enemies.)

3. *What is one way the roadrunner and the quail are different?* (The roadrunner grows to about 22 inches, while the quail grows to about 10 inches; the roadrunner has a long tail, while the quail has a short tail.)

Fluency Score	**Comprehension / Vocabulary Score**	**How to Score Questions**
Total words correctly read in 30 seconds _____ X 2	1. _____ 2. _____	2 = full credit answer 1 = partial credit answer 0 = incorrect/unanswered
Score _____ Goal 61–81 WCPM	3. _____ Score _____ /6 Goal = 4/6	

☐ **Move Ahead** The student met goals for both sections.	☐ **Needs Reteaching** The student did not meet goals for one or both sections.

Space Story

Hona was at her computer. Three moons shined through her window. It was late, but she could not break away from her computer screen. A distant planet was in serious trouble!

It all started with a simple search. She had input "planet" + "trouble" for preliminary research on her school report. Lots of websites had come up, but one really got her attention. It used words like *deep* and *serious*.

Hona was reading an article called "Global Warming Could Prove Fatal." It was about a planet very far away. Hona had never even heard of the planet called Earth.

Hona read on. Suddenly, she called out. "Dad! There's a planet in the Milky Way system that's still using oil for energy! Don't they realize there are other things they can do?"

Suddenly, Mr. Etz appeared in his daughter's room. He read the article. Then he looked up. "Wow! They're close enough to their sun to use its energy! And they have ocean waves, too." He read on. "And wind! Why aren't they using those energies for power? It's so obvious!"

"That's what I'm thinking," said Hona. "Look at this. Their polar ice cap is melting already, and their glaciers, too! I think we should take a spaceship and go over there. Don't you?"

"Absolutely," said her dad. "Get your over-century bag. I'll warm up the spaceship."

Space Story 2

Hona was at her computer. Three moons shined 10
through her window. It was late, but she could not break 21
away from her computer screen. A distant planet was in 31
serious trouble! 33

It all started with a simple search. She had input 43
"planet" + "trouble" for preliminary research on her 51
school report. Lots of websites had come up, but one 61
really got her attention. It used words like *deep* and 71
serious. 72

Hona was reading an article called "Global 79
Warming Could Prove Fatal." It was about a planet 88
very far away. Hona had never even heard of the planet 99
called Earth. 101

Hona read on. Suddenly, she called out. "Dad! 109
There's a planet in the Milky Way system that's still 119
using oil for energy! Don't they realize there are other 129
things they can do?" 133

Suddenly, Mr. Etz appeared in his daughter's room. 141
He read the article. Then he looked up. "Wow! They're 151
close enough to their sun to use its energy! And they 162
have ocean waves, too." He read on. "And wind! Why 172
aren't they using those energies for power? It's so 181
obvious!" 182

"That's what I'm thinking," said Hona. "Look at 190
this. Their polar ice cap is melting already, and their 200
glaciers, too! I think we should take a spaceship and go 211
over there. Don't you?" 215

"Absolutely," said her dad. "Get your over-century 223
bag. I'll warm up the spaceship." 229

GO ON

Name _____ Date _____

Comprehension and Vocabulary Questions

1. *What would be a good title for this story?* (Saving Planet Earth)

2. *What do Hona and her father want to do in the story?* (They both want to help people on Earth find other sources of energy.)

3. *What does Mr. Etz find* <u>obvious</u>*?* (He finds it obvious that the sun, the waves, and the wind are energies that should be used for power.)

Fluency Score	**Comprehension/Vocabulary Score**	**How to Score Questions**
Total words correctly read in 30 seconds _____ X 2	1. _____ 2. _____ 3. _____	2 = full credit answer 1 = partial credit answer 0 = incorrect/unanswered
Score _____ Goal 61–81 WCPM	Score _____ /6 Goal = 4/6	
☐ **Move Ahead** The student met goals for both sections.	☐ **Needs Reteaching** The student did not meet goals for one or both sections.	

La Brea Tar Pits

"Don't touch that! It's dirty and sticky!" Have your parents ever said that to you? Well, maybe someone should say that to a bunch of scientists in Los Angeles, California. Day in, day out, they spend their time digging around in tar.

What are these scientists doing? They are seeking a special kind of bones—the bones of prehistoric animals.

The La Brea Tar Pits sit right in the middle of Los Angeles. So far, over one million bones have been pulled from the pits. They include the bones of mammoths, dire wolves, giant sloths, saber-toothed cats, insects, and birds. Scientists even found some bones from a woman!

How did these bones get there in the first place? Animals might have come bounding into the pits. Then they would get stuck in the tar. They probably grew quite frantic when they realized they were trapped. In time, they would die.

The scientists have the responsibility of taking care of the bones. They are very skilled in what they do. They must be careful when they clean the bones. Some bones are very tiny; others can break easily. Next, the bones are studied and sorted into groups. The clever scientists have ways to date the bones they find. The oldest ones date back 38,000 years! From these bones, we are learning important things about the last Ice Age.

La Brea Tar Pits

"Don't touch that! It's dirty and sticky!" Have your 13

parents ever said that to you? Well, maybe someone 22

should say that to a bunch of scientists in Los Angeles, 33

California. Day in, day out, they spend their time 42

digging around in tar. 46

What are these scientists doing? They are seeking a 55

special kind of bones—the bones of prehistoric animals. 64

The La Brea Tar Pits sit right in the middle of 75

Los Angeles. So far, over one million bones have 84

been pulled from the pits. They include the bones of 94

mammoths, dire wolves, giant sloths, saber-toothed cats, 102

insects, and birds. Scientists even found some bones 110

from a woman! 113

How did these bones get there in the first place? 123

Animals might have come bounding into the pits. Then 132

they would get stuck in the tar. They probably grew 142

quite frantic when they realized they were trapped. In 151

time, they would die. 155

The scientists have the responsibility of taking care 163

of the bones. They are very skilled in what they do. 174

They must be careful when they clean the bones. Some 184

bones are very tiny; others can break easily. Next, the 194

bones are studied and sorted into groups. The clever 203

scientists have ways to date the bones they find. The 213

oldest ones date back 38,000 years! From these bones, 222

we are learning important things about the last Ice Age. 232

GO ON

Comprehension and Vocabulary Questions

1. *Why are scientists digging in the tar pits?* (They are looking for bones.)

2. *What can scientists learn from the tar pits?* (They can learn about prehistoric animals from the bones that are buried there, and important things about the Ice Age.)

3. *How might a <u>frantic</u> animal caught in the pits have acted?* (The frantic animal might have pushed and pulled, desperately trying to get free.)

Fluency Score	**Comprehension/Vocabulary Score**	**How to Score Questions**
Total words correctly read in 30 seconds _____ X 2 Score _____ Goal 61–81 WCPM	1. _____ 2. _____ 3. _____ Score _____/6 Goal = 4/6	2 = full credit answer 1 = partial credit answer 0 = incorrect/unanswered

☐ **Move Ahead** The student met goals for both sections. | ☐ **Needs Reteaching** The student did not meet goals for one or both sections.

A Thanksgiving to Remember

There is one Thanksgiving on the farm that I remember most fondly. It had been an extremely long, hot summer. Then came the drought. If memory serves, it didn't rain for a month straight. Next, the locusts arrived. They were ferocious, eating all plants in their path. And the war raged on, which added to the gloom.

We had a cow, so there was plenty of milk available. Mom thinned out the mashed potatoes by adding butter and cream. Some generous folks brought us food. A small chicken served as a "turkey," and the cabbage had to do as a green vegetable.

We all appeared pretty glum when our dinner was ready, but that would soon change. Just as we sat down at the table, there was a knock on the door. To be helpful, I answered it. There stood my brother, Matt—handsome as a prince in his army uniform. I screamed and jumped into his arms. My shriek was followed by shouts of joy. Soon there was a commotion with everyone squealing and crying. Nobody had any idea that Matt had been released from the army. Now, here he was, safe and sound.

Sometimes I mash my potatoes just like we did that Thanksgiving. I add so much butter and cream that they hardly pile up at all. It brings the memory back.

Name _____ Date _____

A Thanksgiving to Remember   4

There is one Thanksgiving on the farm that I   13
remember most fondly. It had been an extremely long,   22
hot summer. Then came the drought. If memory serves,   31
it didn't rain for a month straight. Next, the locusts   41
arrived. They were ferocious, eating all plants in their 50
path. And the war raged on, which added to the gloom.   61

We had a cow, so there was plenty of milk available.   72
Mom thinned out the mashed potatoes by adding   80
butter and cream. Some generous folks brought us food.   89
A small chicken served as a "turkey," and the cabbage   99
had to do as a green vegetable.   106

We all appeared pretty glum when our dinner was   115
ready, but that would soon change. Just as we sat down   126
at the table, there was a knock on the door. To be   138
helpful, I answered it. There stood my brother, Matt—   147
handsome as a prince in his army uniform. I screamed   157
and jumped into his arms. My shriek was followed   166
by shouts of joy. Soon there was a commotion with   176
everyone squealing and crying. Nobody had any idea   184
that Matt had been released from the army. Now, here   194
he was, safe and sound.   199

Sometimes I mash my potatoes just like we did that   209
Thanksgiving. I add so much butter and cream that they   219
hardly pile up at all. It brings the memory back.   229

Name _____ Date _____

Comprehension and Vocabulary Questions

1. *Why is this a Thanksgiving to remember?* (The narrator's brother came home from war and surprised everyone.)

2. *What important food was not <u>available</u> to the family for Thanksgiving?* (They were not able to get a turkey.)

3. *What can you tell about the narrator's feelings for her brother?* (She loves her brother very much.)

Fluency Score	Comprehension/Vocabulary Score	How to Score Questions
Total words correctly read in 30 seconds _____ X 2 Score _____ Goal 61–81 WCPM	1. _____ 2. _____ 3. _____ Score _____ /6 Goal = 4/6	2 = full credit answer 1 = partial credit answer 0 = incorrect/unanswered
☐ **Move Ahead** The student met goals for both sections.	☐ **Needs Reteaching** The student did not meet goals for one or both sections.	

Trip to the North Pole

In the far north, a group of men struggled against icy wind. It was 60 degrees below zero! The explorers wore thick fur parkas, gloves, and boots. Some thought they should go back. But Robert Peary and Matthew Henson had a pressing need to go on. They wanted to be the first to reach the North Pole.

In 1909, no one had ever been to the North Pole. In the far north, it is light for six months and dark for six months. The team could not cross the ice in the dark. But they would not get any benefit from waiting too long to leave. The summer sun could melt the ice on their way back. Then they would not be able to cross.

The ice in the Arctic often has cracks. These are caused by the pull of the moon's gravity and the movement of Earth. The ice cracks could split open at any time, plunging men into the freezing water. So the team was always prepared to get out of the water and into dry clothes. If they failed, they could freeze to death.

Peary and Henson had tried to reach the North Pole twice before. Both times they had been beaten by the freezing winds, huge blocks of ice, and starvation. Could they make it this time? From their viewpoint, they would not have another chance.

Name ______________________________ Date ____________

Trip to the North Pole 5

In the far north, a group of men struggled against icy 16
wind. It was 60 degrees below zero! The explorers wore 26
thick fur parkas, gloves, and boots. Some thought they 35
should go back. But Robert Peary and Matthew Henson 44
had a pressing need to go on. They wanted to be the 56
first to reach the North Pole. 62

In 1909, no one had ever been to the North Pole. In 74
the far north, it is light for six months and dark for six 87
months. The team could not cross the ice in the dark. 98
But they would not get any benefit from waiting too 108
long to leave. The summer sun could melt the ice on 119
their way back. Then they would not be able to cross. 130

The ice in the Arctic often has cracks. These are 140
caused by the pull of the moon's gravity and the 150
movement of Earth. The ice cracks could split open 159
at any time, plunging men into the freezing water. So 169
the team was always prepared to get out of the water 180
and into dry clothes. If they failed, they could freeze to 191
death. 192

Peary and Henson had tried to reach the North Pole 202
twice before. Both times they had been beaten by the 212
freezing winds, huge blocks of ice, and starvation. Could 221
they make it this time? From their viewpoint, they 230
would not have another chance. 235

GO ON

Comprehension and Vocabulary Questions

1. *What did Peary and Henson set out to do?* (They wanted to be the first explorers to reach the North Pole.)

2. *What dangers did the men face on their trip?* (They faced severe cold, icy winds, cracking ice, and starvation.)

3. *Why was it not a <u>benefit</u> to cross the ice in summer?* (The summer sun would melt the ice, making it impossible to cross.)

Fluency Score	**Comprehension / Vocabulary Score**	**How to Score Questions**
Total words correctly read in 30 seconds _____ <div align="right">X 2</div> Score _____ Goal 82–102 WCPM	1. _____ 2. _____ 3. _____ Score _____ /6 Goal = 4/6	2 = full credit answer 1 = partial credit answer 0 = incorrect/unanswered
☐ **Move Ahead** The student met goals for both sections.	☐ **Needs Reteaching** The student did not meet goals for one or both sections.	

Jenny's Game

Jenny was excited when she finally became a member of the baseball team. Most of the team hadn't wanted a girl to join. But her cousin Roger was an influential member of the team. He knew that she was a great pitcher. So, he convinced the coach that her skill would help them win games. His teammates still had their doubts.

Tonight, after six innings, the team was behind. Jenny watched anxiously, realizing that this might be her chance to pitch. She began to think of a good strategy to use against the other team. Meanwhile, Roger urged the coach to let Jenny pitch.

"What will they think if we send a girl out to pitch?" Jenny heard one player ask.

Suddenly she wasn't nervous; she was angry. Jenny stood up and said, "What will they think if I strike them out?"

"Yeah, give her a try!" another player called. Curiosity was rising. The boys wanted to see what she would do.

When Jenny walked up to the pitcher's mound, there were gasps and then jeers from her foes on the other team. When she threw her own special pitch, there was silence. When Jenny struck out the third player, her teammates cheered as she walked back to the dugout.

Jenny's Game

Jenny was excited when she finally became a
member of the baseball team. Most of the team hadn't
wanted a girl to join. But her cousin Roger was an
influential member of the team. He knew that she was
a great pitcher. So, he convinced the coach that her skill
would help them win games. His teammates still had
their doubts.

Tonight, after six innings, the team was behind.
Jenny watched anxiously, realizing that this might be her
chance to pitch. She began to think of a good strategy to
use against the other team. Meanwhile, Roger urged the
coach to let Jenny pitch.

"What will they think if we send a girl out to pitch?"
Jenny heard one player ask.

Suddenly she wasn't nervous; she was angry. Jenny
stood up and said, "What will they think if I strike them
out?"

"Yeah, give her a try!" another player called.
Curiosity was rising. The boys wanted to see what she
would do.

When Jenny walked up to the pitcher's mound,
there were gasps and then jeers from her foes on the
other team. When she threw her own special pitch, there
was silence. When Jenny struck out the third player, her
teammates cheered as she walked back to the dugout.

2
10
20
31
41
52
61
63
71
80
92
101
106
118
123
131
143
144
152
162
164
172
183
193
203
212

Comprehension and Vocabulary Questions

1. *What does Jenny want to do?* (She wants to join an all-boy baseball team, but the players are against it.)

2. *How do the players feel about Jenny at the end of the story?* (They are surprised by how good she is, and they're happy she is on the team.)

3. *How do you think Jenny's <u>foes</u> feel when she strikes out the third player?* (They are probably shocked and very unhappy.)

Fluency Score	Comprehension / Vocabulary Score	How to Score Questions
Total words correctly read in 30 seconds _____ X 2 Score _____ Goal 82–102 WCPM	1. _____ 2. _____ 3. _____ Score _____ /6 Goal = 4/6	2 = full credit answer 1 = partial credit answer 0 = incorrect/unanswered
☐ **Move Ahead** The student met goals for both sections.	☐ **Needs Reteaching** The student did not meet goals for one or both sections.	

Volcano

We can walk on Earth's outside layer, called the crust, without burning our feet. But the temperature inside the earth is incredibly hot. It's hot enough to melt rock!

As rock below the surface melts, it forms underground pools. More rock melts, adding to each pool. Eventually, solid rock squeezes the pools from all sides. Heat and pressure start to build.

The melted rock pushes upward. If it finds a crack in the crust, it shoots through that opening. As the rock cools on the surface, it begins to form a mound. The mound builds and builds as more of the melted rock pushes out. After much time goes by, a new mountain is formed. This mountain is called a volcano.

A volcano might look like any other mountain, but it is very different. The pool of melted rock remains below the surface. In time, heat and pressure can build up again. Before long, the hot melted rock and gases explode out of the mountain. The volcano is erupting.

Try to get a mental picture of flaming liquid rock shooting out of a mountain. It is truly an amazing sight! But if you want to personally view an eruption, you should do so from a distance. Volcanic eruptions can be extremely dangerous, destroying everything in their path.

Volcano

    We can walk on Earth's outside layer, called the   **10**

crust, without burning our feet. But the temperature   **18**

inside the earth is incredibly hot. It's hot enough to   **28**

melt rock!   **30**

    As rock below the surface melts, it forms   **38**

underground pools. More rock melts, adding to each   **46**

pool. Eventually, solid rock squeezes the pools from all   **55**

sides. Heat and pressure start to build.   **62**

    The melted rock pushes upward. If it finds a crack   **72**

in the crust, it shoots through that opening. As the rock   **83**

cools on the surface, it begins to form a mound. The   **94**

mound builds and builds as more of the melted rock   **104**

pushes out. After much time goes by, a new mountain is   **115**

formed. This mountain is called a volcano.   **122**

    A volcano might look like any other mountain, but   **131**

it is very different. The pool of melted rock remains   **141**

below the surface. In time, heat and pressure can build   **151**

up again. Before long, the hot melted rock and gases   **161**

explode out of the mountain. The volcano is erupting.   **170**

    Try to get a mental picture of flaming liquid rock   **180**

shooting out of a mountain. It is truly an amazing sight!   **191**

But if you want to personally view an eruption, you   **201**

should do so from a distance. Volcanic eruptions can be   **211**

extremely dangerous, destroying everything in their path.   **218**

GO ON ➡

Comprehension and Vocabulary Questions

1. *What does the passage tell you about a volcano?* (It tells how a volcano forms and how it erupts.)

2. *What is the effect of the <u>incredibly</u> hot temperature inside the earth?* (It is so hot that it can melt rock.)

3. *What makes a volcano erupt?* (Solid rock presses on melted rock, and heat and pressure build up inside the mountain, making it explode.)

Fluency Score	**Comprehension / Vocabulary Score**	**How to Score Questions**
Total words correctly read in 30 seconds _____ X 2 Score _____ Goal 82–102 WCPM	1. _____ 2. _____ 3. _____ Score _____ /6 Goal = 4/6	2 = full credit answer 1 = partial credit answer 0 = incorrect/unanswered

☐ **Move Ahead** The student met goals for both sections.

☐ **Needs Reteaching** The student did not meet goals for one or both sections.

The Library Books

Maria hung her head in shame as she entered the library. Her library books were overdue for the third time.

"How careless, Maria!" cried Mrs. Columbo, the librarian. "You have to be more responsible. Somebody might be waiting for one of these books."

"I know," Maria replied. "I forgot all about the books. By the time I remembered, there was no way to get here soon enough. I need to create a reliable invention that can transfer the books back to the library more quickly."

Maria had one zany idea after another. "I could blast the books to the library through a flexible hose," she suggested.

"That might be harmful to the books," Mrs. Columbo observed.

Maria would not admit defeat. "I could build a small plane out of bicycle parts and fly the books to the library."

"That might be harmful to you," Mrs. Columbo remarked. "And do you even have the skills that are required to construct a plane?"

Maria admitted that she did not. Suddenly, a brilliant idea popped into her head. "What if I write a note and tape it to my backpack? That will remind me to bring the books back when they're due."

Mrs. Columbo smiled in approval. "I'm impressed. That's a sensible idea, and you can put it into practice with the books you take out today."

The Library Books   3

Maria hung her head in shame as she entered the   13
library. Her library books were overdue for the third   22
time.   23

"How careless, Maria!" cried Mrs. Columbo, the   30
librarian. "You have to be more responsible. Somebody   38
might be waiting for one of these books."   46

"I know," Maria replied. "I forgot all about the   55
books. By the time I remembered, there was no way   65
to get here soon enough. I need to create a reliable   76
invention that can transfer the books back to the library   86
more quickly."   88

Maria had one zany idea after another. "I could   97
blast the books to the library through a flexible hose,"   107
she suggested.   109

"That might be harmful to the books," Mrs.   117
Columbo observed.   119

Maria would not admit defeat. "I could build a   128
small plane out of bicycle parts and fly the books to the   140
library."   141

"That might be harmful to you," Mrs. Columbo   149
remarked. "And do you even have the skills that are   159
required to construct a plane?"   164

Maria admitted that she did not. Suddenly, a   172
brilliant idea popped into her head. "What if I write a   183
note and tape it to my backpack? That will remind me   194
to bring the books back when they're due."   202

Mrs. Columbo smiled in approval. "I'm impressed.   209
That's a sensible idea, and you can put it into practice   220
with the books you take out today."   227

GO ON ➤

Name _____ Date _____

Comprehension and Vocabulary Questions

1. *What is Maria's problem in the story?* (She has a hard time remembering to return her library books on time.)

2. *How does Maria solve her problem?* (She thinks of different ways to return her books until she decides to just tape a note to her backpack as a reminder.)

3. *Why is Mrs. Columbo impressed with Maria at the end of the story?* (Mrs. Columbo is impressed that Maria finally gets an idea that makes sense.)

Fluency Score	Comprehension / Vocabulary Score	How to Score Questions
Total words correctly read in 30 seconds _____ X 2	1. _____ 2. _____	2 = full credit answer 1 = partial credit answer 0 = incorrect/unanswered
Score _____ Goal 82–102 WCPM	3. _____ Score _____ /6 Goal = 4/6	
☐ **Move Ahead** The student met goals for both sections.	☐ **Needs Reteaching** The student did not meet goals for one or both sections.	

Monarch Butterflies

What has orange wings with black veins and flies? It's a monarch butterfly. As soon as the monarch is transformed from a caterpillar into a butterfly, it's on the move. The monarch can't walk on its spindly legs, but it's an extremely effective flier.

Northern butterflies typically do not migrate both north and south, but monarchs are the exception. They migrate just like some birds. That is, they move from one region to another as the seasons change. In the autumn, monarchs fly south to Mexico. They do not fly alone, but in large flocks of hundreds or even thousands. When the monarchs rest at night, they sometimes cover a whole tree!

When they reach their destination in Mexico, the monarchs spend the winter eating. As spring approaches, the monarchs head back north. However, this time they fly alone. During the trip, the females lay their eggs. The butterflies will die before they reach the place where their journey started the previous year. Their eggs will hatch, and a new generation of monarchs will begin. Their offspring will return to the northern starting point, where they lay their eggs on milkweed plants.

So, the next time you see one of these winged wonders, consider the incredible journey this little butterfly will make. It is a truly remarkable creature!

Monarch Butterflies

What has orange wings with black veins and flies? 11
It's a monarch butterfly. As soon as the monarch is 21
transformed from a caterpillar into a butterfly, it's on 30
the move. The monarch can't walk on its spindly legs, 40
but it's an extremely effective flier. 46

Northern butterflies typically do not migrate both 53
north and south, but monarchs are the exception. They 62
migrate just like some birds. That is, they move from 72
one region to another as the seasons change. In the 82
autumn, monarchs fly south to Mexico. They do not fly 92
alone, but in large flocks of hundreds or even thousands. 102
When the monarchs rest at night, they sometimes cover 111
a whole tree! 114

When they reach their destination in Mexico, 121
the monarchs spend the winter eating. As spring 129
approaches, the monarchs head back north. However, 136
this time they fly alone. During the trip, the females 146
lay their eggs. The butterflies will die before they reach 156
the place where their journey started the previous year. 165
Their eggs will hatch, and a new generation of monarchs 175
will begin. Their offspring will return to the northern 184
starting point, where they lay their eggs on milkweed 193
plants. 194

So, the next time you see one of these winged 204
wonders, consider the incredible journey this little 211
butterfly will make. It is a truly remarkable creature! 220

Comprehension and Vocabulary Questions

1. *Why are monarch butterflies unusual?* (They are always on the move, and they make an incredible journey.)

2. *How are monarch butterflies like birds?* (They fly in large flocks, and they fly south in the fall and back north again in the spring.)

3. *What proof is there in the passage that the monarch butterfly is an* <u>*effective*</u> *flier?* (The butterfly is able to fly great distances as it migrates both north and south.)

Fluency Score	Comprehension / Vocabulary Score	How to Score Questions
Total words correctly read in 30 seconds _____ X 2 Score _____ Goal 82–102 WCPM	1. _____ 2. _____ 3. _____ Score _____ /6 Goal = 4/6	2 = full credit answer 1 = partial credit answer 0 = incorrect/unanswered

☐ **Move Ahead** The student met goals for both sections. | ☐ **Needs Reteaching** The student did not meet goals for one or both sections.

Kate's Surprise

Kate stepped out of the plane into a burst of dry desert heat. Although it was October, it felt like she was walking into an oven. Across the runway, her father waited in the terminal for them to arrive. "I hate this place! I don't want to move here," she thought with a frown. "Why did Dad take this new job? After two months of this stifling heat, I'll be missing New York's December slush!"

Her mother nudged Kate, interrupting her thoughts. "Dad's waving, Katy," her mom prompted. Kate automatically waved back.

Dad undoubtedly looked tan and happy. Maybe in a few weeks she'd look that happy, too. Maybe she'd forget this miserable, lonely feeling. She willed herself not to cry. "Stop it," she reasoned with herself. "You're not a kid anymore—you're practically a teenager!"

After a short drive, Kate exited the car to find herself in front of a one-story house surrounded by cactus plants. "Come around back," Dad said eagerly. "I want to show you something."

"More cactus plants, I bet," thought Kate as she trudged along behind him and thought wistfully about her friends back home.

When Kate stepped around to the back, she couldn't believe her eyes! A great amber-colored horse watched her with curiosity from a corral. "Dad!" she exclaimed in astonished delight, her loneliness suddenly melting away.

Kate's Surprise
                                                                2

Kate stepped out of the plane into a burst of dry   13
desert heat. Although it was October, it felt like she was   24
walking into an oven. Across the runway, her father   33
waited in the terminal for them to arrive. "I hate this   44
place! I don't want to move here," she thought with   54
a frown. "Why did Dad take this new job? After two   65
months of this stifling heat, I'll be missing New York's 75
December slush!"   77

Her mother nudged Kate, interrupting her   83
thoughts. "Dad's waving, Katy," her mom prompted.   90
Kate automatically waved back.   94

Dad undoubtedly looked tan and happy. Maybe   101
in a few weeks she'd look that happy, too. Maybe she'd   112
forget this miserable, lonely feeling. She willed herself 120
not to cry. "Stop it," she reasoned with herself. "You're 130
not a kid anymore—you're practically a teenager!"   138

After a short drive, Kate exited the car to find   148
herself in front of a one-story house surrounded by   158
cactus plants. "Come around back," Dad said eagerly. "I 167
want to show you something."   172

"More cactus plants, I bet," thought Kate as she   181
trudged along behind him and thought wistfully about   189
her friends back home.   193

When Kate stepped around to the back, she couldn't   202
believe her eyes! A great amber-colored horse watched   211
her with curiosity from a corral. "Dad!" she exclaimed   220
in astonished delight, her loneliness suddenly melting   227
away.   228

GO ON

Name _____ Date _____

Comprehension and Vocabulary Questions

1. *Why is Kate unhappy in the beginning of the story?* (She does not want to move to a new home.)

2. *Why is Kate __astonished__ when she sees the horse?* (She is shocked because she never expected such a wonderful surprise.)

3. *How will the horse change the way Kate feels?* (She won't be so lonely anymore.)

Fluency Score	**Comprehension / Vocabulary Score**	**How to Score Questions**
Total words correctly read in 30 seconds _____ X 2 Score _____ Goal 97–117 WCPM	1. _____ 2. _____ 3. _____ Score _____ /6 Goal = 4/6	2 = full credit answer 1 = partial credit answer 0 = incorrect/unanswered
☐ **Move Ahead** The student met goals for both sections.		☐ **Needs Reteaching** The student did not meet goals for one or both sections.

Termites

A tall, brown mound rising from the African savannah looks like a tree stump, but it isn't. It's a termite mound, home to millions of termites. To these tiny residents, the mound seems like a sprawling mansion. Sometimes a termite mound can be as high as twenty feet and can look like a huge sand castle.

The termites build the mound themselves. They mix the soil with their saliva to make sticky glue, which they use to build the mound walls. The hot African sun bakes the walls until they are hard.

The inside of the termite mound consists of a maze of tunnels. Tunnels let in air to cool the termites and to help them breathe. The mound also contains rooms, some of which become storerooms for food. If some mishap occurs and the termites can't find fresh wood to eat, they eat the stored food. Other rooms are nurseries in which young termites hatch and grow.

What happens when the termite eggs hatch in that maze of tunnels and rooms? Some larvae become workers, who do all the work in the mound. Others become soldiers whose only job is to defend the termite colony. Still others become new kings and queens, who leave their "home" mound. On delicate wings they fly away to found new colonies. Soon other termite mounds rise on the savannah.

Termites

A tall, brown mound rising from the African | 9
savannah looks like a tree stump, but it isn't. It's a | 20
termite mound, home to millions of termites. To | 28
these tiny residents, the mound seems like a sprawling | 37
mansion. Sometimes a termite mound can be as high as | 47
twenty feet and can look like a huge sand castle. | 57

The termites build the mound themselves. They mix | 65
the soil with their saliva to make sticky glue, which they | 76
use to build the mound walls. The hot African sun bakes | 87
the walls until they are hard. | 93

The inside of the termite mound consists of a maze | 103
of tunnels. Tunnels let in air to cool the termites and | 114
to help them breathe. The mound also contains rooms, | 123
some of which become storerooms for food. If some | 132
mishap occurs and the termites can't find fresh wood to | 142
eat, they eat the stored food. Other rooms are nurseries | 152
in which young termites hatch and grow. | 159

What happens when the termite eggs hatch in that | 168
maze of tunnels and rooms? Some larvae become | 176
workers, who do all the work in the mound. Others | 186
become soldiers whose only job is to defend the termite | 196
colony. Still others become new kings and queens, who | 205
leave their "home" mound. On delicate wings they fly | 214
away to found new colonies. Soon other termite mounds | 223
rise on the savannah. | 227

GO ON

Name _____ Date _____

Comprehension and Vocabulary Questions

1. *What would be a good title for this passage?* (A Great Home for Termites)

2. *Why might the mound seem like a sprawling mansion to the termites?* (The termites are so small that the tall mound probably seems so spread out to them.)

3. *What is a termite mound like on the inside?* (It is a maze of tunnels and rooms.)

Fluency Score	**Comprehension / Vocabulary Score**	**How to Score Questions**
Total words correctly read in 30 seconds _____ X 2 Score _____ Goal 97–117 WCPM	1. _____ 2. _____ 3. _____ Score _____ /6 Goal = 4/6	2 = full credit answer 1 = partial credit answer 0 = incorrect/unanswered

☐ **Move Ahead** The student met goals for both sections. ☐ **Needs Reteaching** The student did not meet goals for one or both sections.

Pizza Party

The fans cheered enthusiastically when Central's basketball team fulfilled their goal of winning five games in a row. The team had struggled all year, but now they led their division. Teammates Shawn and Billy wanted to celebrate the victory by going out with their friends. It was late, though, so Shawn's parents proposed that everyone come to their house to celebrate.

"We can have pizza," Shawn's father suggested, "if it's all right with everyone's parents."

"That's an awesome idea, Mr. Potter!" Billy replied.

While Shawn's father went to get his minivan, the other team members asked their parents for permission to attend the pizza party. Billy, Krista, and Jordan, who all lived nearby, got a ride with Mr. Potter. Those who lived further away planned to come with their parents.

On the way home, Mr. Potter picked up two large pizzas. The first to appear at Shawn's house were the identical twins, Nick and Ray. They arrived with their father, who was carrying two extra-large cheese pizzas. Shortly, the car pool from Jefferson Street made an appearance. Alex, Jamal, and Nicole each carried a large, flat box in their hands. The enticing aroma was unmistakable—pepperoni pizza.

"What's happening here?" Shawn's father asked, amazed at the number of pizza boxes.

Shawn and his friends couldn't believe their eyes. "We're hungry, but not that hungry!" they laughed.

Name _____ Date _____

Pizza Party 2

    The fans cheered enthusiastically when Central's 8
basketball team fulfilled their goal of winning five 16
games in a row. The team had struggled all year, but 27
now they led their division. Teammates Shawn and Billy 36
wanted to celebrate the victory by going out with their 46
friends. It was late, though, so Shawn's parents proposed 55
that everyone come to their house to celebrate. 63

    "We can have pizza," Shawn's father suggested, "if 71
it's all right with everyone's parents." 77

    "That's an awesome idea, Mr. Potter!" Billy replied. 85

    While Shawn's father went to get his minivan, the 94
other team members asked their parents for permission 102
to attend the pizza party. Billy, Krista, and Jordan, who 112
all lived nearby, got a ride with Mr. Potter. Those who 123
lived further away planned to come with their parents. 132

    On the way home, Mr. Potter picked up two large 142
pizzas. The first to appear at Shawn's house were the 152
identical twins, Nick and Ray. They arrived with their 161
father, who was carrying two extra-large cheese pizzas. 170
Shortly, the car pool from Jefferson Street made an 179
appearance. Alex, Jamal, and Nicole each carried a 187
large, flat box in their hands. The enticing aroma was 197
unmistakable—pepperoni pizza. 200

    "What's happening here?" Shawn's father asked, 206
amazed at the number of pizza boxes. 213

    Shawn and his friends couldn't believe their eyes. 221
"We're hungry, but not that hungry!" they laughed. 229

Name _____ Date _____

Comprehension and Vocabulary Questions

1. *If the team* <u>struggled</u> *all year, how well did they probably play?* (The team was having trouble and probably not winning most of their games.)

2. *What is the reason for the pizza party?* (The team just won five games in a row, so they are no longer struggling.)

3. *What happens in the story to make everyone laugh?* (Everyone picks up pizza on the way to Shawn's house—so now they have too much pizza!)

Fluency Score	Comprehension/Vocabulary Score	How to Score Questions
Total words correctly read in 30 seconds _____ X 2 Score _____ Goal 97–117 WCPM	1. _____ 2. _____ 3. _____ Score _____/6 Goal = 4/6	2 = full credit answer 1 = partial credit answer 0 = incorrect/unanswered
☐ **Move Ahead** The student met goals for both sections.	☐ **Needs Reteaching** The student did not meet goals for one or both sections.	

Ferris Wheels

Ferris wheels are fun rides used at carnivals, fairs, and amusement parks. The typical Ferris wheel stands 40 to 50 feet high and carries 20 to 30 people. This giant rolling wheel is quite an impressive sight. But when was it created, and who came up with the idea?

The Ferris wheel was introduced at the World's Columbian Exposition in Chicago in 1893. This wheel was built by a bridge maker named George W. Ferris, who got the idea by looking at the structure of a merry-go-round. The structure had to be adapted so it would function upright. Ferris's plans called for a vertical wheel that would make every other wheel look small. The wheel was 250 feet in diameter. It had 36 cars that carried a total of 2,160 people. Previously, there had been no ride built on such a grand scale. This huge wheel was used again in 1904 at the St. Louis exposition.

You might think that the height of Ferris wheels would cause them to tip over easily, but there have been few accidents involving them. The wheels can withstand winds of 60 miles per hour. Also, owners are continually checking the rides to make sure they are properly maintained.

Not as thrilling as roller coasters, Ferris wheels are for those who want a more relaxing ride with a wonderful view.

Ferris Wheels

Ferris wheels are fun rides used at carnivals, fairs,   11
and amusement parks. The typical Ferris wheel stands   19
40 to 50 feet high and carries 20 to 30 people. This giant   32
rolling wheel is quite an impressive sight. But when was   42
it created, and who came up with the idea?   51

The Ferris wheel was introduced at the World's   59
Columbian Exposition in Chicago in 1893. This wheel   67
was built by a bridge maker named George W. Ferris,   77
who got the idea by looking at the structure of a merry-   89
go-round. The structure had to be adapted so it would   100
function upright. Ferris's plans called for a vertical   108
wheel that would make every other wheel look small.   117
The wheel was 250 feet in diameter. It had 36 cars that   129
carried a total of 2,160 people. Previously, there had   138
been no ride built on such a grand scale. This huge   149
wheel was used again in 1904 at the St. Louis exposition.   160

You might think that the height of Ferris wheels   169
would cause them to tip over easily, but there have been   180
few accidents involving them. The wheels can withstand   188
winds of 60 miles per hour. Also, owners are continually   198
checking the rides to make sure they are properly   207
maintained.   208

Not as thrilling as roller coasters, Ferris wheels   216
are for those who want a more relaxing ride with a   227
wonderful view.   229

GO ON

Name _____ Date _____

Comprehension and Vocabulary Questions

1. *Where could you see a Ferris wheel?* (Ferris wheels are found at carnivals, fairs, or amusement parks.)

2. *What is a Ferris wheel?* (It is a large wheel with cars that people can ride in. It can hold up to thirty people at a time.)

3. *The Ferris wheel was part of the St. Louis exposition. Where was it seen <u>previously</u>?* (It was first seen at the World's Columbian Exposition in Chicago.)

Fluency Score	Comprehension / Vocabulary Score	How to Score Questions
Total words correctly read in 30 seconds _____ X 2 Score _____ . Goal 97–117 WCPM	1. _____ 2. _____ 3. _____ Score _____ /6 Goal = 4/6	2 = full credit answer 1 = partial credit answer 0 = incorrect/unanswered

☐ **Move Ahead** The student met goals for both sections.	☐ **Needs Reteaching** The student did not meet goals for one or both sections.

Jake Does the Dishes

Jake groaned when his father asked him to do the dishes. Of all his chores, this was the one he disliked the most. Every time he washed the dishes, some disaster occurred. Undoubtedly, today would be no exception.

"The sooner I get this over with, the better," Jake reasoned with himself. With a sigh, he walked to the kitchen and began to run hot water in the sink. He didn't notice that a spoon was lying in the sink, just under the faucet. Immediately, water splashed off the spoon and splattered all over the walls. Jake just grimaced and continued.

Then Jake began to squirt dishwashing liquid into the pan, but the bottle bounced from his wet hands. Dishwashing liquid shot out, leaving a sticky mess around the sink. Another sigh escaped from Jake's throat.

Jake continued on, reaching for a stack of dinner plates sitting on the counter. As he reached, his shirtsleeve caught on the handle of a skillet. The skillet shifted, bumping into some saucepans and lids. The pans and lids crashed to the floor, making a tremendous clatter. Little splatters of food from the pans lay all over the floor.

At that moment, Jake's father, hearing the racket, ran to the kitchen door. When he saw the incredibly helpless expression on Jake's face, he broke into laughter.

Jake Does the Dishes

Jake groaned when his father asked him to do the dishes. Of all his chores, this was the one he disliked the most. Every time he washed the dishes, some disaster occurred. Undoubtedly, today would be no exception.

"The sooner I get this over with, the better," Jake reasoned with himself. With a sigh, he walked to the kitchen and began to run hot water in the sink. He didn't notice that a spoon was lying in the sink, just under the faucet. Immediately, water splashed off the spoon and splattered all over the walls. Jake just grimaced and continued.

Then Jake began to squirt dishwashing liquid into the pan, but the bottle bounced from his wet hands. Dishwashing liquid shot out, leaving a sticky mess around the sink. Another sigh escaped from Jake's throat.

Jake continued on, reaching for a stack of dinner plates sitting on the counter. As he reached, his shirtsleeve caught on the handle of a skillet. The skillet shifted, bumping into some saucepans and lids. The pans and lids crashed to the floor, making a tremendous clatter. Little splatters of food from the pans lay all over the floor.

At that moment, Jake's father, hearing the racket, ran to the kitchen door. When he saw the incredibly helpless expression on Jake's face, he broke into laughter.

4
14
26
35
42
52
62
73
84
91
101
104
112
122
130
136
139
148
157
167
175
185
196
198
206
216
224
225

GO ON

Comprehension and Vocabulary Questions

1. *What always happens when Jake does the dishes?* (Jake has a disaster when he washes the dishes.)

2. *Why does Jake have so much trouble washing the dishes?* (He doesn't pay enough attention to what he is doing.)

3. *Do you think that some disaster will <u>undoubtedly</u> occur every time Jake washes the dishes?* (Answers: Yes, because Jake is too careless; No, it can be prevented if Jake is more careful.)

Fluency Score	**Comprehension/Vocabulary Score**	**How to Score Questions**
Total words correctly read in 30 seconds _____ X 2 Score _____ Goal 97–117 WCPM	1. _____ 2. _____ 3. _____ Score _____/6 Goal = 4/6	2 = full credit answer 1 = partial credit answer 0 = incorrect/unanswered

☐ **Move Ahead** The student met goals for both sections. | ☐ **Needs Reteaching** The student did not meet goals for one or both sections.